# Christy

### The Story of a 'Greyt' Greyhound

*Cassandra*

Anyone who lives in New Hampshire and would like to adopt a Greyhound can contact:

**Greyhound Placement Service**
Michele Houghton
432 6th St, Dover, NH 03820
(603) 842-4349
michelle@k9kaos.com
www.adopt-a-greyhound.org

For all other states please research where your regional Greyhound adoption agency is to contact.

*Thank you!*

Disclaimer: The early events in this book from Christy's birth to her arrival at the Greyhound Placement Service are all the speculative imagination of the author. However, the events that begin with the introduction of Cassandra and Carmen are true.

This publication and its characters are protected by copyright. Unauthorized reproduction, distribution, or transmission in any form or by any means, including photocopying, recording, or other electronic or mechanical methods, is strictly prohibited without prior written permission from the publisher. Limited quotations in reviews and certain noncommercial uses permitted by copyright law are exempted.
All rights reserved.

Paperback ISBN: 979-8-9899836-2-9
Hardcover ISBN: 979-8-9899836-3-6

©2024 Copyright Cassandra
All Rights Reserved
Printed in the United States of America

The e-book maintains the original design of the print edition, ensuring that all elements are fixed in place. Readers can easily zoom in and enlarge the content using the pinch and zoom functions while previewing in landscape mode.

All images are the property of Cassandra
Edited by Margaret Williams - Thank you!
Interior and cover design - Lisa Monias

Carmen          Richard

# Dedication

In loving memory of Maria del Carmen Garcia Cortes, a.k.a. "Aunt Karmie," and Richard Earl Damman.

A big thank you to my heavenly Abba for all His gifts to me. And to Eric for your love and belief in me!

I love you!
Cassandra

| CHAPTER 1 |

# BIRTH

It was a frigid winter morning on December 4, 1992, when former racing greyhound Rikasso Bunny circled nervously around her homemade den. The puppies inside of her were making it known more and more that they wanted to be born.

She let out a low whimper and plopped down with a sigh on a warm blanket. It would only be a matter of minutes now until her sons and daughters entered the world. She then laid her head down and pushed.

"Daddy, look! Bunny had her puppies! There are four of them, and they are so cute!" eight-year-old Christy Bernadone shouted excitedly. Her green eyes sparkled with wonder as locks of brown hair fell across her small forehead. A strong hand from behind her grasped her right shoulder with affection.

"Yes, Christy, isn't it wonderful? They will be fine dogs just like their mother," Mr. Bernadone replied.

"Can we keep one this time Daddy? Please?" the beautiful girl pleaded.

"Now honey, you know that this is our business and that they will be going to the track to earn money. We're not in this for pleasure," Mr. Bernadone reminded his daughter. Christy frowned in sadness. "But you can name them all just like before. I promise."

With that Christy smiled a little and said, "OK Daddy."

The two stood there a bit longer, watching as Bunny licked her four small puppies dry and nudged them to where they could fill up on delicious milk. She seemed not to notice the eyes watching her as her puppies wriggled with closed eyes, pawing each other and at their mother's belly. Their small ears flopped down over their heads making them look comical. But one day they would be graceful and athletic racing dogs.

Bunny continued to lick her puppies. They knew they were loved.

| CHAPTER 2 |

# GROWTH

Time marched on, and the newborns became larger puppies. Every day they ran and played in the yard, growing the strong muscles they would need to help them run at great speeds on the racetrack. Mr. Bernadone eyed each one carefully hoping soon one, if not all, would be winners of many races, just like their father Black Streaker.

There was a white male with one big brown spot on his back that Christy named Streakin Hydro. Another male was brown with a large white spot on his back, the opposite of his brother. This one Christy named Streakin Dynomite. Their sister was completely white. Christy named her Streakin Flash. And then there was the last sister. She was a fawn color, a light goldish yellow with four white feet and a white tip on her tail. Her brown eyes were friendly and loving. She was sleek and the favorite of Christy but still without a name. As she ran in the yard one day Mr. Bernadone and Christy watched in amazement at how fast she ran.

"She's like a streak of light. I bet she will be a winner one day," Mr. Bernadone exclaimed with a smile.

"Daddy, can we name her Streakin Christy? If I can't keep her, at least she can be mine in name. I think it fits her perfectly!" Christy pleaded as she jumped up and down.

Mr. Berndadone grinned widely.

"Sure, honey, Streakin Christy it is!"

"Yaaaaaayyy!" Christy cried happily as she twirled around in circles.

The newly named Streakin Christy wagged her tail and barked in agreement. Father and daughter laughed hard. It was a happy moment for all of them.

| CHAPTER 3 |

# NEW LIFE

All too soon fourteen months had passed by, and it was time for Streakin Christy and her brothers and sister to go to the racetrack to learn how to be a racer. With tears in her eyes, the now nine-year-old Christy hugged her favorite dog.

"Goodbye Streakin, you be a good girl and win lots of races for Daddy and me! You know I won't be able to come see you race because I'll be in school, but you'll be in my heart," Christy said sadly.

Her dog whined several times, somehow sensing that something was wrong, as she had never seen her cry before. Mr. Bernadone then came over with a leash and snapped it on her collar, then handed the leash to a friendly looking man with an Irish accent.

"Thank you, Joe, I know you'll take good care of them. Let me know about their progress," Mr. Bernadone said.

"Aye, don't worry about a thing. They'll be in good hands," Joe responded as he led Streakin Christy away to a van filled with her brothers and sister. He put her into a crate so she wouldn't get hurt during the ride, then shut the back door. He then started the van to begin the one-hour drive to the racetrack.

A few days went by and Streakin Christy still wasn't sure about this new place. It made her nervous as it was filled with many other greyhounds besides her and her family, who constantly barked until nighttime. She also wasn't used to being locked up for twenty-two hours at a time in such a small area. The only times she was let out was to train and to be groomed.

Although Joe was good to her and came several times a day to take care of her, she still wished for something different. She missed the young girl who used to give her kisses and hugs and pats on the head. She missed the play time she had in the yard, with her brothers and sister. There they were free! But now they had all entered the training phase of their lives. Suddenly Joe appeared in the kennel carrying two buckets and a scoop. He approached her crate and opened the door.

"There you go lass. Eat it all so you can have energy for training in the morning!" he said as he dumped a bucket of meat into her steel dish, then stroked her head in affection before closing her door.

## NEW LIFE

Streakin Christy quickly devoured her dinner, licking her lips and hoping for more. When she had finished her meal, she eyed her brothers and sister in the crates in front of her, wishing she could be with them freely again. In sadness she whined, circled a few times around her small crate, then plopped down heavily to sleep. Soon all the barking ceased as forty hungry hounds quickly filled their stomachs with their meal.

| CHAPTER 4 |

# THE TRACK

"That a girl! Chase the rabbit! Good girl!" Joe shouted to Streakin Christy as she ran at full speed around the dirt track. It was her third time out here for training and she was beginning to really enjoy it. She learned that when she was muzzled it was time to go outside and be placed in a box. Then when the front of the box opened, she was to dart out and chase the mechanical rabbit on the rail. But that was the best part! For that was when she was free! Free to run like the wind like she did in her puppy days. Free to run as fast as her slim legs would let her. She ran and ran and ran to her heart's desire, joy swelling up in her. This is what she was born to do!

But all too soon the rabbit would stop suddenly. Streakin Christy and all the other hounds she trained with would slide to a halt and try to get it. But the muzzle on her face never let her. Quickly Joe would run up behind her to snap the leash on her collar and pull her away back to her crate for a rub down. Her fun was over for the day.

"Good girl, you ran a great time today! You'll be ready for your first race next week lass," Joe said happily. Streakin Christy wagged her tail at the upbeat tone of Joe's voice. Her training was now over. It was time to race.

| CHAPTER 5 |

# RACEDAY

"It's a beautiful day here folks as the dogs enter the track for the first race at Lakes Region Greyhound Park. Get your bets in early and avoid being shut out at the window! Ten minutes to the start of race one," the track announcer said over the loudspeaker.

Streakin Christy had known somehow that today was going to be different when Joe came into the kennel to feed that morning, but he had skipped her. She had also been weighed twice and given extra attention to her feet and nails. Now a blanket with the number eight was being attached around her belly. Joe then put her muzzle on and leashed her. He then led her out onto the track where she saw seven other greyhounds being led around by their handlers too. Many people filled the once empty grandstands as seagulls glided overhead. The laughter of three children soon caught her attention as she turned to see if Christy the girl with the beautiful green eyes and brown hair was there. But she was not.

"Pay attention lass. You've got to run really fast for us today and make us some money," James sang to her. His voice focused her attention back to the track in front of her. She was being led to the familiar black starting box. But today wasn't a training exercise. She had to run to prove something now.

Into the box she was shoved, the last to go in. Her muscles tingled with the excitement she could sense. Suddenly a bell rang, the front of the box was raised and the words, "They're off!" rang through the air.

Streakin Christy shot forth like a rocket and was in full stride within a second, running alongside her competition. She then realized the mechanical rabbit was missing. It was just her and the others free to run as fast as they could. In a few more seconds she was in fourth place!

However, in the next ten strides she got boxed in on the rail by the other hounds with no room to go around the hound in front of her, or to the side. It didn't matter though because she was running, and she loved it!

The pack ran tightly together towards the last turn before the finish line. Streakin Christy still couldn't move out of her position. Suddenly a large spotted male rammed her on her right shoulder, causing her to trip and fall! She tumbled head over heels to the ground, biting her tongue in the process. The other hounds flew by her in a blur to finish the race in a few more strides. Streakin Christy slowly rose to her feet as blood poured out of her mouth. A three-inch cut also bled from her right shoulder. Joe ran to her quickly with a concerned look on his face.

"Oh, my poor lass! What a terrible event you've just had! Let's get you back to the kennel and have the vet take a look at you," Joe offered gently as he patted her head in comfort.

Streakin Christy walked slowly back to the kennel in pain, her tongue hanging out of her mouth revealing a small split at the top. She was then led into a room she had never been in before. She trembled in fear as she was picked up and laid on a cold metal table. A man in a white overcoat entered the room and put something fluffy in her mouth.

"It's ok pretty girl, I'm just trying to stop your tongue from bleeding and then I'll fix your shoulder cut," the track vet said in a calming voice. Streakin Christy sensed he was trying to help her, so she stopped trembling. Joe stood next to her, stroking her sleek face. He silently wondered if she would have the courage to race again.

| CHAPTER 6 |

# TRY AGAIN

Two weeks passed, and Streakin' Christy recovered well from her injuries. Her cut shoulder now bore a permanent pink scar that would never grow hair again, a forever reminder of her racing days. Her tongue also remained split, but it wasn't sore anymore. However, whenever she panted her tongue curled perfectly around a front tooth, which added to her uniqueness.

"Ok lass, it's time to get you back in training so you can race again!" Joe happily sung to her one morning as he opened her crate to muzzle her. But she knew what the muzzle meant and turned her head away to avoid it. Joe was surprised at this, so he cradled her face in his hands to slip the muzzle on.

"Now lass, no sense in fighting this, once you get on the track and start running, you'll remember how much you love to do it. Let's go," Joe said encouragingly.

Streakin Christy reluctantly jumped out of her kennel and slowly followed her handler.

Once on the track she was glad to see it empty, as her accident was still fresh in her memory. She was then hurriedly put into the starting box and went through her training like before. She ran a little slower than usual, but Joe still greeted her with a smile on his face.

Two days later Streakin Christy was entered in her second race. She ran as fast as she could as she headed towards the last turn before the finish line. Just as she was about to dart through a hole that had opened in front of her, a spotted male came into her sights. It was him, the same hound who had slammed her before! In fear she suddenly slowed down and let him pass her, hoping he wouldn't slam her again. Then the race was over.

Streakin Christy finished last.

| CHAPTER 7 |

# RACE ON!

Another week passed until Streakin Christy was entered in her third race. She knew she had lost the last race when Joe had no kind words for her, but only a pained expression on his face. It was just that she had been afraid and didn't want to get hurt again. But today she would try to be a brave girl!

Onto the track she went and into the starting box. The now familiar bell rang and the shout of "They're off!" echoed in her ears, as she shot forward at great speed.

Going around the first turn she had managed to move into third place. Knowing she was close to the front, her heart pounded with excitement and joy at the thought that she could be the winner. But then out of the corner of her eye she saw a blur of black and a white spot. No, it couldn't be, yet it was him again! He ran up alongside her and tried to pass her, laying his ears back to cause fear. It almost worked as Streakin Christy thought about stopping again, but she wanted to be brave so she decided she would have none of this boy's threats and surged ahead with every fiber of her being.

In two strides she had passed him just as the finish line whirred by. Streakin Christy came in third! Her heart was joyous as she was greeted by loving words and pats on the head from Joe. Her number was then placed on the board. The people who had bet money on her were happy they had won their money back.

"What a great gal you are my lass! You showed that ol' boy, didn't ya?" Joe laughed.

Streakin Christy walked back to her kennel wagging her tail and holding her head high. The spotted male walked back with his tail hanging low as well as his head. He knew he had been defeated.

| CHAPTER 8 |

# RETIREMENT

Streakin' Christy went on to race several more times, but no matter how fast she ran, she could never win a race. Mr. Bernadone paid for her racing career as long as he could. But she wasn't winning any money to cover the expenses, so he had no choice but to retire her from the track. And since it was his policy to never keep the dogs he raced, he decided to let her go to a greyhound adoption agency in Goffstown, New Hampshire, where she could find a new forever home.

So, on a sunny day in March 1995, Streakin Christy (now just called Christy), was loaded onto a van by Joe. Inside were four other greyhounds who had also been retired from racing by their owners. After a two-hour ride, Christy was received kindly by a lady named Michele. She would take care of Christy and find her a forever home. She was placed into a kennel just as at the track. Here there were fifteen other greyhounds also waiting for new homes. At least she would not be lonely.

Life was good at this adoption kennel. Michele treated Christy as if she were her own dog. She was allowed to run a couple times a day in a big back yard with a few of the other hounds. Still, she longed for something more. She wanted to be free and to be loved as she was by the beautiful little girl she was named after. She hoped that day would come soon.

Several weeks passed and many people came in and out of Michele's kennel to look over the different greyhounds for adoption. However, no one chose to take Christy home. She even learned how to quiver her jaw and make her teeth chatter as a cute trick to get attention. Even so, no one wanted Christy.

More weeks went by as did the people in and out to choose their next friend with Christy still hoping for her own family. Still, no one wanted the silly dog with the split tongue and scar on her shoulder.

Then one day, two ladies came into the kennel with Michele. Christy recognized them for they recently had been coming every few days to walk a brindled colored male. They went as usual to him, opened his crate and put a leash on him.

"Hi Boss! How's my boy?" the younger lady said happily.

Boss wagged his tail in happiness. Christy looked intently at them, hoping they would notice her this time and take her out, too.

# RETIREMENT

"Who do you want to walk today, Carmen?" Michele asked the older lady.

Carmen looked at each dog and finally came to Christy. Christy knew this was her chance and started to quiver her jaw and chatter her teeth. Carmen started laughing.

"Oh Precious, look at this dog, she's chattering her teeth!" said Carmen in a Spanish accent, while motioning to her niece Cassandra, (who was nicknamed "Precious" by her deceased mother Martha).

"Wow, that's really funny! Hey Michele, what is this dog's name?" Cassandra asked.

"That's Christy; do you want to take her?" Michele asked.

Carmen nodded her head yes, so Michele opened Christy's crate and leashed her.

"Here you go, have a good walk," Michele said handing the leash to Carmen.

Christy's tail wagged a mile a minute, she was finally going out for a walk!

How great it was to see the sunshine and all the new things around! There was a field and abandoned railroad tracks. There were squirrels and birds and mice and grasshoppers. But most of all there were these two nice ladies who kept petting her and telling her what a pretty girl she was. Boss walked beside her, nosing her and licking her face several times.

"Awww... they like each other. I'll have to ask more about her," Cassandra said.

When they returned to the kennel Michele was waiting for them.

"What's the story on this Christy dog? Cassandra asked. "Boss licked her face and gave her kisses."

"Oh, they play together in the yard, they're best buddies," Michele answered.

"Oh, I can't separate them if they're buddies. Can I adopt her, too?" Cassandra asked.

"Sure you can. She's still available," Michele said with a smile.

"Great! I'll come get them this weekend!" Cassandra said happily.

So it was now official. Christy had a home!

| CHAPTER 9 |

# A NEW HOME

Two days later Christy was waiting in her crate with a wagging tail when Cassandra and Carmen came to take her and Boss home. Michele wasn't there, so Christy wasn't able to say goodbye to her. None the less, Christy was happy to go.

Carmen went to her crate and opened the door. She leashed her and told her to jump down. Christy did with quivering jaw, which made Carmen laugh.

Cassandra took Boss out of his kennel. Then they were led outside and motioned to jump into the back of her SUV. They happily did so.

About half an hour later they arrived at a tan house, where they were let out of the SUV. Christy and Boss panted in excitement. Could Christy's dream really be coming true? Was this going to be her forever home?

They were led inside the house and unleashed. Never being off a leash inside a house since she was a puppy, Christy was a little anxious about what to do next. Cassandra patted her and encouraged her.

"Go on girl, look around, this is your new home!" she said happily.

Christy and Boss started to sniff around cautiously, investigating every comer and room with a wagging tail. This was all new to them.

"Boss, Christy! C'mon babies!" Carmen called out.

Upon hearing their names, they came running to a sliding glass door that was opened for them. They ran through the opening and into a large backyard filled with plush green grass! Immediately Boss started to run in circles, prompting Christy to join him. They chased each other in happiness around the lone tree in the comer for ten minutes before plopping down on the ground in exhaustion. The grass felt cool underneath them as the hot May sun shone brightly on them.

What freedom! What beauty! No more being locked in a kennel for twenty-two hours a day! No more racing, no more heartache! This is what Christy (and Boss!) had always hoped for and now it was true.

Cassandra and her Aunt Carmen sat down on the grass next to them and patted their panting sides. Suddenly Boss lifted his head and got up. He wanted to run some more! Christy not wanting to be left out, got up, too, and started to run with Boss again.

Round and round the yard they went at incredible speed. Suddenly Boss headed for a bench that was near the left side of the fence. In a graceful leap Boss jumped over it. Christy seeing Boss do it decided she would try and jump over the bench too. Up she went, but oh! Her left hind leg got caught, and down she crashed in a yelp of pain.

"Oh Christy! You poor girl! You're not as graceful as Boss I guess!" Cassandra cried out as she ran to her.

Christy trembled in her arms. "C'mon, let's get you to the vet!"

So once again Christy went to see the man in the white coat.

| CHAPTER 10 |

# THE FAMILY

A few hours passed when Christy and Cassandra finally returned home. The vet had done x-rays which showed Christy had three small bone chips and a pulled tendon in her left hind leg. However, the vet did not want to operate and said it would be best to leave the leg alone. Cassandra felt terrible that in the first hour of bringing her home Christy had gotten a permanent injury.

After she led a limping Christy into the house, a happy Boss greeted her at the door licking her face with kisses. He had missed his girlfriend!

Cassandra's stepfather Richard also lived in the house but had been sleeping this whole time. He was a retired postal worker who was going blind and was suffering from heart disease, so Cassandra and Carmen took care of him. Now he was awake and eager to meet the new additions to the family.

"Hi Christy, hi Boss!" Richard said as he patted them on their heads.

They sniffed his hands curiously, learning his scent so they would recognize him in the future.

"Want a cookie?" Richard asked holding out two dog biscuits.

Christy and Boss sniffed them trying to figure out what they were. Boss gently took it into his mouth and started to crunch. Christy, upon seeing this, snapped the biscuit out of Richard's hand. Their tails wagged in enjoyment.

"Here you go," Richard said as he handed them two more. Boss took his gently as before but Christy eagerly snatched hers again out of his hand.

"Wow, you gotta watch that Christy, she's a snapper!" Richard laughed.

Christy wagged her tail in agreement.

"Looks like you made some friends Dad!" Cassandra exclaimed.

"Yeah, they're beautiful. I haven't had a dog around in forty years," Richard commented with tears in his eyes. He was very happy to have more companions in his last days.

Sensing his emotions, Christy licked his hand. Boss wagged his tail and looked at Richard with soulful eyes, begging for another cookie. And of course, they both received one, with hundreds more to come over the years.

THE FAMILY

As their first day of freedom came to an end, Christy and Boss curled up on the couch, one on each side like bookends. They slept in peace; happy they finally had a forever home!

| CHAPTER 11 |

# A NEW ADVENTURE

Life for Christy and Boss in their new home was great. Christy's leg healed as best as it could, only causing her to limp slightly a few steps after rising in the morning. None the less, it never stopped her from running every day in the backyard with Boss.

Christy and Boss took possession of the couch, the loveseat, all the beds as well as every inch of floor. Every hour they changed their sleeping location, feeling confident that this was indeed their forever home. The cookies were abundant as well as the attention and love. Retirement was great!

One day though, Cassandra only took Christy outside the front door and put her in the SUV to go for a ride. Christy whimpered a little, not liking to be separated from Boss. After half an hour she let Christy out and led her into a building she had never been in before. It had strange smells and lots of different noises which made her afraid. Christy started to whine until Cassandra patted her side and made her feel better.

"It's OK Christy, you'll like this," Cassandra comforted her.

Christy was then led to an elevator and urged to get on. However, she had never seen anything like it before and refused to go in by planting her feet firmly on the ground. Cassandra had to push her in from behind. When the doors closed and the elevator began to rise, Christy braced her feet. Within seconds the ride was over, and the doors opened onto the floor of a nursing home. A very eager Christy walked off the elevator.

"What a brave girl you were!" Cassandra said in a praising voice.

Christy wagged her tail in response.

At this nursing home were many people who couldn't take care of themselves anymore because of their age, illness, or an injury. So, they lived there, and were cared for by nurses and aides. Cassandra herself worked at this nursing home as a nurse's aide. She then led Christy over to a group of three elderly women sitting in rocking chairs who looked very sad and lonely.

"Hello ladies, want to pet a dog?" Cassandra asked.

The three immediately started to smile and pet Christy all over.

"What a beautiful dog! What kind is she?" one lady asked.

"She's a greyhound that is retired off the racetrack. I adopted her a few weeks ago," Cassandra replied with a smile.

"What's her name?" the second lady asked.

"Christy," Cassandra replied.

"She's lovely. She reminds me of a dog I had when I was younger, and my husband was still alive," the third lady said with tears in her eyes.

"Hi, Christy," the ladies said as they continued to pet her.

Christy, loving the attention, kept putting her head under their hands to get more pettings. Soon many other residents of the nursing home saw Christy and started coming over to pet her and ask questions. They all had smiles put on their faces.

Cassandra led Christy around to meet many people who all loved seeing her and petting her. Christy sensed she was bringing something special into the lives of these poor people who were filled with pain, loneliness, and the boring routine of nursing home life. Her tail wagged nonstop as she planted kisses on everyone.

After an hour Christy was led back to the elevator for it was dinner time for the residents. But this time Christy was brave and walked onto the elevator without hesitation. Cassandra knelt and took Christy in her arms. "What a special girl you are Christy. You made so many people happy today!" Cassandra said with pride.

CHRISTY

    Christy wagged her tail and licked her face. She was indeed a special girl.

| CHAPTER 12 |

# ESCAPE!

The weeks passed by, and Christy and Boss settled into the routine of life. Their different personalities became clearer as they felt more secure in their new home and let themselves come out of their shell.

Christy loved to squeeze her head in between your knees and have her butt scratched while she wiggled back and forth like she was dancing. Her tail would wag a mile a minute. She would pull her head out to bark at you to do it again. Then she would shove her head in between your knees for a repeat scratch.

She also loved to push against Richard's legs and direct him to where the cookie jar was. She would bark until you gave her one to take outside, called a 'cookie out'. When she came back in the house, she would go to the jar and bark for her 'cookie in'. Her plan always worked with Richard, and soon Boss became wise to the plot and joined in. Then Richard would have both dogs pushing on his legs directing him to the cookie jar!

Christy loved to give kisses, kisses, and more kisses. She would lie down next to you on the couch and put her paw on your lap.

Christy and Boss also became so in tune with each other that on several occasions they were found to be lying in the same exact position except facing opposite directions, which earned them the nickname 'the bookends'. It was very amazing to see, and everyone wondered how they knew how to do that!

Yes, their life was good and very ordinary until one Saturday afternoon.

Cassandra and Carmen had gone out shopping. Richard was in the driveway talking to two men about repairing a fence. He opened the garage door and showed them they could get into the backyard through another door in the back of the garage, making it easier for them to bring in the fencing materials.

As Richard started to go back into the house he said to the men, "Just remember to close both the back door and garage door when you leave so the dogs don't get out."

"Ok," they replied as Richard entered the house.

An hour or so passed and the two men finished their work and left. Christy and Boss whined to go outside so Richard let them out. Ten minutes later Richard called for them to come back in, but they did not.

They were gone!

Richard strained to see with his nearly blind eyes at what could have happened. Then he realized the two men had forgotten to close the front and back doors in the garage, so the dogs had walked right out.

He went to the front porch and called for them, but they were nowhere in sight. Richard felt bad because he couldn't drive to go look for them. Sadly, he closed the door knowing he had no choice but to wait for Cassandra and Carmen to come home. (This was before cell phones!). Richard could only hope they would be alright.

| CHAPTER 13 |

# FREEDOM!

Wheeeeee! This was so much fun! Christy and Boss ran quickly down the steep hill to the bottom of the street where the neighborhood ended, and a sidewalk began. The smell of hamburgers hung in the air, coming from a restaurant across the street. So, they decided to dart across the busy four lane road ignoring the horns blowing at them. They ran into the parking lot where the restaurant was. Both wished they could get a sample of the tasty smell but adventure waited and there was a whole world out there to see! On they ran next into a field behind the restaurant.

They mouth wrestled with each other, chased each other in circles and explored for quite some time before continuing to the other side of the field, where a hill led down into a river.

There they jumped into the cool water splashing each other in fun. Now this was really freedom!

They played and played and played until the sky suddenly started to turn dark. Big clouds rolled in overhead and thunder was heard nearby. A storm was coming! Sensing the storm, Christy started to whine, not knowing what to do. She started to become nervous and turned to get comfort from Boss, but he was gone! She barked for him but there was no reply. She cried, whimpered, howled, and moaned but still there was no Boss.

The rain suddenly began to fall heavily, and Christy quickly became drenched. She hung her head low and walked into a wooded area where she found a tall bush to lie under. There she closed her teary eyes. Why had Boss left her? Now she was lost and on her own. She whimpered for Boss, for her dinner, for Cassandra, Carmen, and Richard, and for her dry and warm home. How had she gotten into this? She hoped her family would soon find her.

After about two hours the storm stopped, and the sun started to come back out. Christy, still soaking wet, rose to her feet and shook her body. She looked around hoping Boss had come back, but he had not.

She tried to remember the way her and Boss had taken and started to climb up the hill that led across the river and back into the field. She slipped and scratched her paws a couple of times on the rocks since they were wet. When she finally reached the top and crossed the river, the field was before her. She barked a couple times still hoping for Boss, but he did not answer.

So she ran across the field and ended up back at the restaurant and ran happily into the parking lot. There she recognized the hill they had come down across the street, so without thinking, she dashed across the road! Suddenly brakes squealed and a horn blew as Christy was almost hit by a truck. This caused her to freeze in fear as a van sped by in the next lane, it's horn blaring at her. When it had passed by, she leapt forward into two more lanes of traffic. The sound of screeching tires filled the air which panicked Christy now into a frenzied run.

Within seconds she was on the sidewalk again where several people had stopped to try and to catch her. but she ducked away from them with speed. Then she darted up the hill to where she thought her neighborhood was where there were rows after rows of houses. Now if only she could find the tan house that was her home! Christy became excited and started to trot up and down the streets.

Around and around, she went until she was confused. She had not recognized her home at all! She sniffed the ground trying to pick up a familiar scent, but it was no use. This was not her neighborhood.

Christy spent another hour going through this strange neighborhood. Many people called to her, but she ignored them. All she wanted were the loving arms of her owners.

"Hey Mark, look! A greyhound!" a young boy called out to an older one. They were both holding water pistols.

"Wow, perfect target practice. Let's get it," yelled the older boy as he started to aim and shoot streams of water at Christy.

Christy yelped in surprise when struck with the water and started to trot away, but the boys ran after her.

"We're gonna get you!" they screamed at Christy as she started to run away in a panic around a corner.

A turning car almost hit her again, but stopped to yell at the boys when the driver realized what they were doing.

Christy kept running in fear until she was several blocks away from the boys. When she couldn't run anymore, she stopped and breathed heavily. She found a tree in a wooded area and slowly walked over to it and laid down in the shade. She started to whine again, really wanting to go home. She had had enough of freedom!

There Christy stayed for hours, napping, and dreaming of Boss and her playing in the backyard. Oh, how she wished she were there right now! More time passed and a sad Christy waited under the tree. She tried to sleep again but a sound caught her ear. Faint at first but it got closer and closer, and it was familiar!

"Christy! Christy! C'mon girl!"

It was the voice of Cassandra! She was slowly driving her SUV up and down the streets calling for her. In a second she turned the corner and was driving right past Christy. However, Cassandra's face was turned the other way.

"Christy!" she called out again.

Christy stood up and let out a loud bark.

Cassandra turned her head and then spotted her.

"Christy!" she cried out excitedly.

Christy ran to the SUV and jumped up onto the driver's side door, her tail wagging a mile a minute. Cassandra quickly put the SUV in park and got out to hug Christy tightly. Tears were streaming down her cheeks.

"Oh Christy, where have you been? We've been so worried about you!" She said in a choked voice.

Christy licked her face repeatedly and wagged her tail.

"C'mon girl, get in," she said as she opened the hatchback where an eager Christy jumped in. She was finally going home!

| CHAPTER 14 |

# THERE'S NO PLACE LIKE HOME

Christy was surprised when the ride home only lasted two minutes. She had ended up in the neighborhood next to her own. If only she had taken a right at the bottom of the hill instead of a left! Cassandra then pulled into the driveway of her familiar home.

"Now we have to find Boss, he's still missing, and no one has called about him," Cassandra said sadly.

Christy cocked her head trying to understand the words.

Christy was let out of the SUV and was about to walk towards the front door when a vehicle pulled up in front of the house. It was the Police Animal Control van for stray dogs. Peering through the bars in the back of the van was a very guilty looking Boss. A policewoman stepped out of the van.

"Did you lose a greyhound ma'am?" She asked with concern.

"Oh yes! A door was left open by some hired workers and he escaped!" Cassandra answered anxiously, hoping Boss wasn't going to be taken away.

"Ok, I won't give you a ticket this time, but try not to let it happen again," the policewoman said as she opened the back of the van. Boss eagerly jumped out and ran excitedly to Cassandra with his tail wagging a mile a minute.

"Boss! Oh, my poor Boss! Where did you go!?" Cassandra exclaimed. Christy, seeing her buddy, ran up to Boss and started to lick his face. Boss just stood there and leaned up against Cassandra's leg for security.

"Thank you!" She called out as the van started to pull away. The policewoman waved in acknowledgment with a smile on her face. She was happy that the dog had been returned home safely, instead of being taken to the pound where an uncertain future awaited many unclaimed dogs.

"Well, I wonder what you two did!" Cassandra laughed. Boss and Christy wagged their tails.

"Yeah, I bet you had a lot of fun, Next time leave a note, ok? C'mon. Let's go see Aunt Karmie and Pop!" she said, as she eagerly opened the front door.

Richard was sitting on the couch with outstretched arms waiting to greet "the children."

"Hi guys, where have you been? I thought you were gone forever," Richard said with tears in his eyes.

Carmen then came into the house from the back porch.

"Awww... babies!" she cried happily as they raced next to see her.

"Boss was arrested and brought home in the paddy wagon," Cassandra laughed.

"Oh, you are a bad boy Boss?" Carmen joked.

Boss replied with a bark.

They all laughed together in happiness for their reunion.

That night Boss and Christy stuck by each other and followed whoever happened to be up and walking about. They ate two bowls of dog food each, and suckered Richard out of a full bag of dog cookies. At night Christy slept at the foot of Richard's bed, and Boss slept on top of Cassandra's feet. It was good to be together again.

# CONCLUSION

Six years went by, and Richard passed away in April 2001 from kidney failure due to diabetes. Carmen also passed away in September of 2001 due to a heart attack.

Cassandra sold the house they had all lived in together. She got married to an awesome man named Eric and moved to the country in northern New Hampshire. There Eric and Cassandra bought a home with 9 acres where Christy and Boss could run freely and enjoy their remaining two and a half years of life.

Then on a sunny hot day in July 2003, a 12 ½ year old blind Boss and 11 ½ year old Christy, suffering from arthritis, crossed the Rainbow Bridge to return to their Heavenly Creator. They were buried at home in front of a statue of St. Francis of Assisi.

They had many more adventures in the time they were with Cassandra and Eric including getting loose one more time, until they were found in a gravel pit half a mile away from their home! They brought much happiness to Cassandra and Eric.

Boss was gentle, quiet and a funny boy.

Christy was outgoing, energetic and an affectionate girl.

Together they were 'Greyt' greyhounds!

# ABOUT THE AUTHOR

Cassandra resides in North Texas with her husband, 2 cats and 2 dogs. She's a member of the Third Order Franciscans who loves to relax by reading and stargazing.

*Cassandra*

Contact: authorcassandra@protonmail.me

www.thirdorderfranciscans.com

Christy and Boss

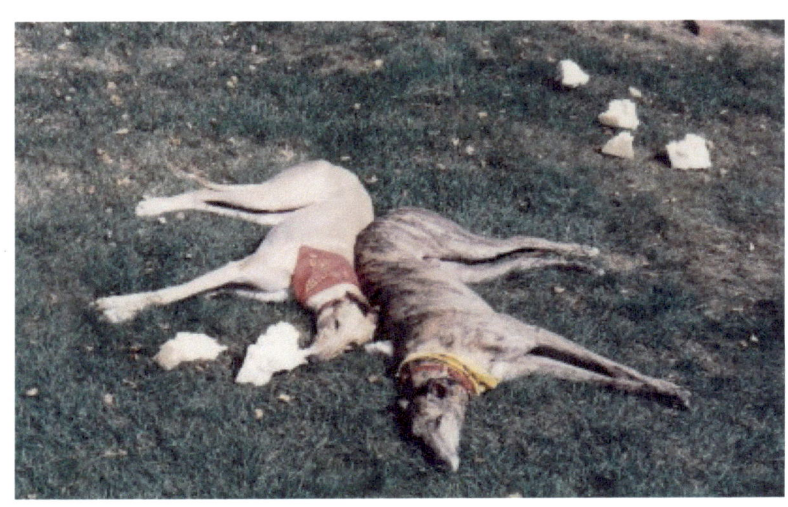

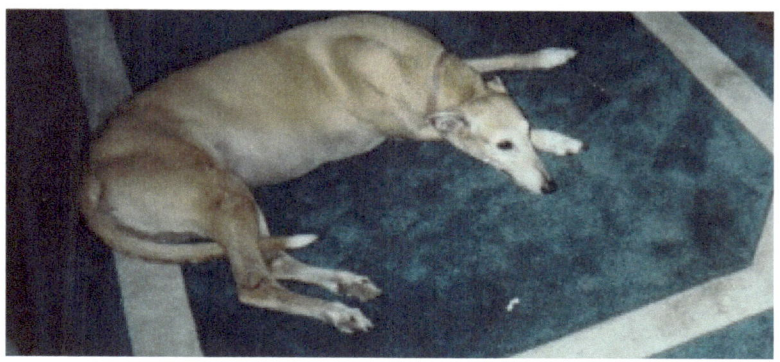

www.ingramcontent.com/pod-product-compliance
Lightning Source LLC
Chambersburg PA
CBHW040732060526
44119CB00078B/287